T0209194

Journaling Through Awakening

An Inner Voyage to the Remembrance of Who You Are

Vince Alexandre

BALBOA.
PRESS
A DIVISION OF HAY HOUSE

Balboa Press books may be ordered through booksellers or by contacting:

Balboa Press
A Division of Hay House
1663 Liberty Drive
Bloomington, IN 47403
www.balboapress.com
1 (877) 407-4847

Print information available on the last page.

ISBN: 978-1-9822-1194-3 (sc)
ISBN: 978-1-9822-1195-0 (e)

Balboa Press rev. date: 09/19/2018

Dedicated to all the awakening souls of this Earth who are in search of themselves and of their true home. I have deep compassion for you all and I love you. I hope this book will find you when you need it, and will provide you with many life-changing insights.

I would like to send all my appreciation to Janet for spending hours with me editing this book, absolutely for free. Your knowledge of the English language is impressive, and your compassion for me and my story have touched my heart deeply. You've been an amazing friend to work with.

I would also like to deeply thank, in no particular order: John, Yan, Annick, Nelson, Ianik, Pauline and Jason for their financial contribution to this project. Thank you for believing in me. Your support means the world.

And last but not least, a massive thanks to my parents and family for having been there in tumultuous times and for being a light when life feels dark.

PROLOGUE

My name is Vince Alexandre, I am 25 years old and I come from a small town in Canada.

I have lived there most of my life. In 2012, when I moved to one of our country's largest cities, to explore something new in my life, I strongly felt the calling to spread my wings and reach out for greater opportunities.

March 2013 is a time that I will never forget. It marked the beginning of my spiritual journey. However, it was not all rainbows and roses. My awakening started very abruptly on a day like any other. What I was about to go through would surpass anything that my mind could comprehend at that time.

I've been wanting to write this book for a long time now, but the timing was just not right. I still had to gain a bit more wisdom in order to put into words the message I wanted to share. When I was about 11 years old, I told my mom: "Someday I'm going to write a book, and it will touch people's lives." However, I did not know that I would be the main character in my story.

I feel so honored and blessed to be a part of your Earthly experience. Know that I've put my heart and soul into this book, and it is my wish that the sparks of love it radiates will ignite a fire in you - the sacred fire of your divinity.

Each and every one of us has talents, passions and interests. When we break free from the constraints of our society and pursue those passions with confidence, we bless the world with the love of God. By following the calling inside of our hearts, devoting ourselves to trusting the divine and allowing our boundless potential to flow, we light up the day of every individual who crosses our path. This is what the world needs right now.

Most of you will relate in some way to the story you are about to read, no matter where you stand on your personal path. There is something for everyone in this book. Whether you have been exploring a spiritual journey for a while or are just awakening, know that you will receive insightful advice that will benefit you for a lifetime. Though the circumstances we experience may vary largely, they all point in the same direction and serve the same purpose - to make us remember who we truly are.

You are not your body. You are not a simple reflection in the mirror. You may have a glimpse of your essence in the stars of your eyes, but who you truly are has more depth and is more magnificent than anyone has permitted you to believe. You are here on Earth at this moment because you are on a very important mission, and we are on that mission together. I am here to help you remember.

It is no coincidence that you have stumbled upon this book today and felt the urge to read it. There is a reason you were guided to pick it up at this particular time. One of the things I have learned is that there are no "coincidences" in God's plan. What there are are perfectly orchestrated Divine circumstances, synchronicities. Unfortunately, many people will instantly discard such truth without even questioning themselves, because of the false beliefs they have been fed in the past by the predominantly closed-minded society we live in. If only each one of us would take a moment to reach inside his or her heart and listen to what the heart says. We are all able to differentiate lies from truth.

The title of this book, "Journaling Through Awakening" came from a vision. After my massive awakening, I felt urged to write a book that would help other people going through a similar situation. When I searched for the name, two ideas appeared in my mind, either: "Journeying" or "Journaling" Through Awakening. I was not sure yet which one I wanted to use. It was when I started to collect some of my writings from past years that it became so evident.

During this process, I started to meet new friends in a variety of groups gathered through the use of the Internet. These new friends were going through an experience similar to mine. I then felt safe to share my daily experiences with them and to get insights.

I have included some of my Internet postings in this book and kept them as raw as possible to give you examples of what I experienced in my daily life. I am not here just to show you the pretty side of spiritual development, but all sides of this process to give you a broader perspective. Still, I always try to find the positive, the silver lining through it all. You are not alone. You are already perfect as you are and free to move forward with confidence. The main goal of this book is to assist you in awakening to your truth.

If you feel uncertain about what tomorrow will bring, if you seek answers or if you can relate to the feeling of having collided with a force greater than yourself, then you have the right book in your hands. I know what you are going through, because I have been through it myself, and I am still learning something new everyday. Life is always teaching.

I hope that this book will open for you new horizons and that the teachings you learn will benefit you for a lifetime. Welcome to the inner voyage to the remembrance of your Divine Nature.

CONTENTS

CHAPTER ONE

Just a Small Town Boy

Besides coming from a very small town, I am also an only child. I was blessed to be raised in a loving family, well sheltered by my parents and four grandparents. I realize that not everyone has had this chance, and I am very grateful for this gift. For the most part, I sailed smoothly on the waves of life during my early years. The only other young child in my neighborhood lived across the street, and sometimes I would call him and we would play video games together. I would spend much of the rest of my time alone, in my own world. I am not complaining because I was happy that way. I did not feel lonely, for my imagination was profusely abundant. Still today, I tend to be selective with regard to the people I choose to spend time and energy with in my daily life, although I'm friendly and I always enjoy connecting with like-minded souls.

Institutions, especially school, never suited me. Even though I often got the highest marks in my class and was loved by my teachers, I just wasn't happy there. When kindergarten started, the thought of leaving my mother terrified me. As if my terror wasn't enough, I broke a leg two weeks before the beginning of classes and had to start school one month after all the others. Making friends was difficult since social circles had already been established. I felt excluded. I would spend most of the day crying to go back home, and my teacher became exhausted. No matter how hard she tried, there was nothing she could do the relieve my agony.

Nothing could alleviate the sadness, pain and suffering I was feeling, just by being there. Being surrounded by all those children, in that context, felt awkward to me. Even though I was a very loving child and sociable most of the time, I didn't like the way school was organized. I didn't like the feeling of being trapped. I did not have the awareness or the vocabulary to pinpoint and express what I was feeling.

Now that I think about it, this has been a major theme in my life. I've always longed for freedom and refused to stay where my heart felt caged. I'm a free spirit, a creator, an artist, and I need to express myself positively, otherwise I don't live. I just exist. Today I understand that even though that early childhood phase was painful to me, everything happens for the purpose of our soul's growth. Difficult experiences are to be embraced and forgiven. Each one has brought us closer to our Divine self.

The intensity of the situation got milder during elementary school as I somehow found a way to mold myself to society. However, it wasn't long before things started to go downhill, and this, prompted, for the first time, a spiritual calling inside me.

Coming from a small town, my uniqueness was not always warmly welcomed. When I arrived in high school, an infernal cycle of bullying started. I was bullied because of my sexual orientation, even though at the time, I was still trying to discover who I really was. I was shocked to be ridiculed for something I hadn't yet figured out for myself. Little did I know that being the only guy in a group of girls and having spiked, dyed hair, was enough to put a bull's-eye on my back.

Even though certainly not everyone had my worst interests at heart, it felt as if it were everyone when the same groups of guys tormented me regularly. The hurt doesn't have to be physical to cause damage. The emotional and psychological pain was unbearable. This went on for about two years, the first year being the most intense year of suffering. Every morning when I arrived at school, I did not know what to expect, and this put me in a state of constant fear and anxiety.

Today, I do not hold on to any hard feelings and have forgiven all those who hurt me intentionally or not during that time. We have all been someone's persecutor or abuser at one point or another. With the spiritual understanding I have now, I know that all is part of Divine order. No matter the situation, we are always teaching each other a lesson of love, even though it may not feel like it at first. It is important to remember that this life is a playground where we all play roles in each other's lives, so things need not be taken too much to heart, not too seriously.

CHAPTER TWO

Coming Out...of the Dark Era

We are coming out of a dark era, a time when we have exchanged love, cooperation, harmony and peace for fear, selfishness, disruption and chaos. This dark state of mind is reflected in many spheres of society.

Think about your daily life. Are you feeling deeply fulfilled, passionate and enthusiastic about what your life has become? Are you listening to your heart's calling? Are you living up to your heart's desires or have you settled for less, somehow believing that "life is what it is" and that you can't do anything about it? Instead of turning a blind eye to a reality you don't want to see, it's time to face the truth and take action. Sitting on the sidelines and doing nothing is also a choice! It is time for you and I to take our destiny in our own hands, so that the qualities of unconditional love are restored within ourselves and the world - so that all that represents fear fades away.

If we take, for example, the bullying problem in schools, I think it's relevant to ask: "Where did these young people learn such rough judgements against others?" And it's not just regarding sexual orientation, anyone who doesn't fit the mould is subject to harassment. Where does this behaviour of destruction come from?

Everyone should feel safe, especially in the environment where they grow and learn.

Even though the bullying issue is also a part of life, especially in the workplace, I'm going back in time to illustrate a point. Every adult was once an innocent and loving child, free from judgement. Unable to protect himself from the thousands of thoughts with which he is bombarded with everyday and that are coming from multiple sources, the child absorbs them as a sponge would. Each negative thought deepening limiting and restrictive patterns.

What we see in our schools and in the society, in general, is the refection of eons of prejudices. I believe that no one is born bad. Even those who challenge our light serve God. In God's eyes, there is no "right" or "wrong". These are human perceptions. I'm definitely not suggesting that we should do hurtful things and not expect that the lesson will come back to us - because it will - I'm just saying that different souls have different paths, and all have their part to play in God's plan.

If you are dissatisfied with your life circumstances right now, that's because you have gone through some kind of conditioning and unconsciously or consciously accepted lies as truths. The goal is not to find out who is guilty, but to know that you have the power to change anything that no longer resonates with your truth.

At some point, it is our responsibility to decide what kind of life we want to experience and what message we want to send out to the world. Maybe we couldn't help ourselves as children, maybe we didn't know any better at that time, but now everyday is a new opportunity to choose. You are not a passive victim. You have the awareness and free will to make conscious and deliberate actions for the betterment of your own life and that of others.

Now is the time to release all the negative energy you've been holding on to and to start living the life you were meant to live! We are all the masters of our own creation. If we allow the darkness of our past to hinder us, we must face the consequences that come with that choice. It is not what I want for you, not what I would want for myself.

At some point, I had to make the choice that I would let go of all resentment and hurt, because they would otherwise have bound me to a victim mindset. We don't attract what we want, we attract what we vibrate. That is why it is so important to release old constraints.

When I started to follow my vocation for spiritual healing and teaching, I wasn't sure if I needed to share the fact that I am gay. I am aware that many people, depending on their backgrounds, will react differently to this information. However, it became clear to me that if I am to fully undertake my Soul's mission and shine my light to the fullest, I have to be transparent with who I am and not just show those parts of my identity that are already socially accepted.

Depending on where you are in your spiritual journey, some of the themes I am going to discuss in this book might feel a little uncomfortable to you, but always remember that the discussion is meant in a loving way for the purpose of helping you break through preconceived notions.

Ultimately, I am who I am, and I am happy with the decisions my Soul made before incarnating as me. I wouldn't change anything, no matter the struggles. These struggles have made me the person I am today. I now understand that they had a specific purpose in my growth and I am therefore grateful for each experience.

CHAPTER THREE

Making Sense of this Existence

When I was young, I knew I had a great mission. I could feel inside my heart that I was here to help others. I did not know how to make this happen, but I knew I would make it happen somehow.

The superficiality of our day and age has never made much sense to me, and I have always longed for some deeper sense. From what I could see, growing up, the view seemed so limited that I just wanted to fly far away among the stars and never come back. It was a daily process to be at peace with myself and my surroundings. It still is today. However, it becomes easier when you realize that in spiritual truth, you play many roles all at the same time and that, no matter what, your unbounded Soul, your essence, remains unchanged.

If you've gone through much of your life believing that what you physically see is all there is, then maybe you could now take some time out and start questioning yourself in order to see beyond limited horizons. Learn to listen to your own heart instead of believing everything others say.

Don't you feel deep inside that there is something more to life than just what you can see? Do you believe that your greater calling in life consists only of working a dead-end job to pay the bills and then sinking in a black void for eternity? As I write these couple last words, my heart feels so constricted that I know it can't be true! Have you ever asked yourself these questions?

We tend to become so engulfed in old paradigms because of the way we are conditioned throughout our lives by various sources that we continue to participate in a reality that no longer resonates with our beliefs nor serves us. Maybe we've been so conditioned not to listen to our hearts and Souls that we're not able to hear them? Well not anymore. It's about time we shake things up for the better.

There is so much more to existence than just what meets the eye. When we cross over in Heaven, we remember what reality is, but the goal is to awaken and remember while we are still here in physical form. There is no "void" after we leave this plane. You "are" right now, and you still "are" after you've transitioned. You cannot possibly stop existing. The spark of consciousness that you are can't vanish.

You came here to experience this part of creation, but there is so much more happening at the same time on other levels of your existence. While you're here, you have to discover and fulfill your missions, both on a personal and global level. We each need to find our Soul's purpose.

"I am the man as well as the Divine. I am both the personality evolving through human stories and the higher intelligence, in this moment in time. I honor my existences gracefully & peacefully, for, above all, I am Soul observing through the universal eye of the One."

I remember a particular day when I was a student. I had some spare time between two classes. I wasn't living the present moment back then; I was impatiently waiting for the end of the day, the weekend, vacations. I viewed happiness as something that was to be found outside of myself, as if there were conditions that needed to fall into place before a state of contentment and joy could be reached. On that day, in a moment in between classes, I went into a bathroom and had an existential crisis. I was tired and fed up with my life. I looked outside through the very small window and said to God: "I can't believe that this is all life has to offer. I can't believe there isn't something more than this! I don't want to be here anymore, I want to go home!" Even if I didn't know what "home" was, where it was, or how to get there...

Many of us, lightworkers, struggle at some point with that sense of not belonging to this Earth. We feel that something doesn't quite "add up" here and we want to return to our Source. This happens because when we incarnate into this dimension, we forget the Divinity that we are and what we came here to do. This is all done on purpose for our Soul's growth, and it is our task in this life to remember.

As we advance in our development, however, we understand that home is in the heart and that no matter where are currently experiencing life, it is possible to live in love most of the time. It is a matter of vibration, instead of location. To realize this, one must dig deep within and transmute all the old programming that is no longer positively aligned with his or her truth. That takes a lot of courage, but in my experience, living in denial is far more unbearable. So I followed my heart and the result is the goal of this book - to encourage and prompt you to do the same.

When I realized that in every moment, each of us makes a choice about how he is going to experience life, a whole new world of possibilities opened in front of me. I went from seeing the world in black and white, to living in color.

My crisis that day inspired a poem. Here is "World of Dreams".

"World of Dreams"

Take me to a distant land,
Where birds float free
All I need is a caring place to lay my heart
Let it soar, be.

My skies were fading grey,
When you came around and asked me to stay.
You held my hand and told me to look up
You said: "You are the shining star in my midnight sky."
My heart beat faster;
Your eyes were brighter than ever.

The wonder of the wind carried us
Jolted sparks of love everywhere
We danced together in harmony
With gravity undone.

Life's never what it seems
But for a moment we got lost in a beautiful world of dreams.
We held each other tight
And turned darkness into light.
Our hearts knew
That for the loved one they had to surrender the past
And make every second, here, this moment, last.

Take me to a distant land
In your steady hands I lay my heart,
Soaring, happy.

CHAPTER FOUR

Depression... A Blessing in Disguise

Recently, I stumbled upon a quote that resonated with me. It said that being depressed is actually a state of "deep rest." I thought it made so much sense!

When I was going through that state myself because of the bullying I had experienced, I was beyond tired of existing. I didn't want to die, I simply didn't want to "be" anymore. It was more than just sadness. I was experiencing emotional and spiritual pain to an extent that was unbearable, and I wanted the pain to vanish.

I did not find excitement in anything, and even the simplest task looked like a mountain to climb. I had no interest in relationships whatsoever and spent much of my time secluded, it was a difficult state to overcome. At that point, I hadn't yet learned how to let go of my past, and these old, outdated and unnecessary thoughts kept replaying in my mind, attracting more deceitful situations in my life.

When we learn to let go, we do not define ourselves by our past anymore, and we become free from the suffering related to painful memories. I will talk more about karma clearing in the upcoming chapters, a safe way to free you from your past. This is such a basic principle that it could easily be taught to children at a young age in schools!

If you have experienced depression in the past or are currently going through this condition, know that I have deep empathy and love for you. I know exactly what it feels like because I went through it myself several times. Advancing through daily life seemed empty and pointless. This happens when you ignore your Soul's calling, your deepest yearnings and live in the past. May a thousand angels surround and comfort you in their healing light, and I extend my spiritual arms to wherever you are to help alleviate the pain you are feeling. It is a phase to a better tomorrow. You will not stay sad forever.

Experiencing my first depression at the age of 16, I started to look for remedies other than pharmaceutical that would lead to a path of recovery. I started to look online for self-help programs and started to explore my mind in the hope of finding some solutions.

At my lowest point, I had to use medication, and it did serve its purpose, but I knew that just masking the symptoms wouldn't bring me the deep inner sense of peace for which I was longing. I knew that I had to dive deeper to treat the root of the problem. Psychotherapy helped, but still, the results weren't long lasting in my case. What was it that was missing? I had no clue, but I was determined to keep pushing and find out for myself.

That's where my spiritual quest started, and I can now say that the depression was a blessing in disguise...

CHAPTER FIVE

The Aftershock

What you are about to read might shock you, but it is not my intention to frighten you. This is what I experienced, and no one goes through a process in the same way as another. We are all entitled to our own paths in life and things can happen for reasons that may not be clear at any one time. What I'm talking about is the "spiritual awakening" that many of you probably already know since you have felt inclined to read this book.

Even though it was apparent to the adults around me that I was not like the other children in some way when I was younger; my childhood was not particularly marked by psychic experiences. Thinking back however, I realize that I did experience some, but they felt pretty normal to me.

I remember one night, I was at my grandma's house, and she had a beautiful framed picture of Mother Mary and Jesus on her wall. I was lying on the bed, and the faces on the picture started moving and talking to me. I did not hear words or sounds, but the faces were clearly moving and their expressions were meant for me. I didn't question myself much at the time, but now that I reflect on that experience, it was "unusual" and interesting.

Another night, I was home, sleeping in my bed, and I woke up from a dream. I looked to the left side of my bed and saw a little boy in white light standing there. This surprised me and without knowing what I was doing, I closed the connection. I was afraid. Later, I questioned what I had experienced and convinced myself that it must have been my imagination. However, I still remember the scene to this day, and I now know that these phenomena are not only possible, they happen and they are real. As a child, I also often felt as if I were being followed. I could feel presences around me almost as if they were chasing me, but again dismissed them.

In my teenage years, I started meditating. Once during meditation, I saw and felt small white shapes swirling around me, and elevating me, my energy. Another time, I was visited by what looked like a red dragon. I was in deep meditation, and focusing on the ceiling, when a long red shape flew over me. Interestingly enough, I later received a channeling from a lightworker who mentioned a similar creature.

During these years, I remember looking at my reflection in a mirror or window, focusing for long periods of time and seeing my face and body completely vanish. I became bodiless at these moments, so to speak. I felt energized and uplifted afterwards.

It's also around that time that I saw faces appearing in my mind when my eyes were closed, and I was ready to go to bed. I saw all kinds of different faces - from young to old, beautiful to scary. This annoyed me greatly as it prevented me from resting. I asked one of my few spiritual friends at the time, how to stop this. I did what he suggested and the faces eventually disappeared. My friend's suggestion that I call on the angels, freed me of the appearing faces and motivated me to find out more about these loving beings of the Light. However, it was not until the age of 19, when I was faced with the most difficult and horrifying phase of my life, that I really understood the importance of protecting my energy.

I believe that everything happens for a reason and that I have experienced life in such a way that will allow me to share my story with others. I hope that they can relate in some way, find inspiration, discover new knowledge.

So now, let me share with you how I experienced an awakening. But first, let me put some elements in context for you.

In September of 2012, I moved away from home. It was quite a change. I thought to myself that it was finally my chance to start living a brand new life in a big city. My main motivation was to pursue my studies in communications and discover more of the world, to challenge my beliefs.

Maybe it was a little bit naive on my part. It's as if I believed that somehow I could just put the hurt from my past in a drawer at the back of my mind and never look back. The truth is, it's not by escaping our past, but by letting it flow through us - and ultimately, out of us - that we are able to finally release it.

My first semester went pretty well. I had to adjust to many different aspects of life, but I was mostly satisfied with how things unfolded. My grades were good, and I met new people. I enjoyed the independence of living in an apartment for the first time.

My awakening phase started in January of 2013. By that time, I had become greatly interested in spiritual matters, especially because of the highly mediatized "End of the World" that was "supposed" to happen on December 21st, 2012. My curiosity was piqued, and I would spend hours online, sorting through various resources on the subject and trying new meditations to expand my heart and mind. That's when I was introduced to "ascension" for the first time. It wasn't so long ago, yet so much has changed since then.

What happened next, is that I met with an acquaintance who offered to smoke a joint of pot with me. I don't recommend using alcohol and drugs, because I've seen the havoc that can be created in a person's life. Nevertheless, I agreed. I guess I wanted to escape this reality, and that's exactly what I did, but not in the way I had planned.

Before I go further, I want to specify that my intent is not to condemn the use of cannabis. Many are advocates for this plant's healing proprieties, and some use it as a prescribed treatment for their condition. I respect everyone's journey. I believe that because I'm an extremely sensitive person, mind-altering substances have a stronger effect on me, so I prefer staying away from those. We ultimately all have free will and what works for someone is not necessarily suited for someone else. We are all entitled to our own path. However, remember that you don't need a substance to open the doorway to your heart. You may do so naturally.

What happened to me is that this one joint triggered a kind of psychosis, but more than that, it induced a major trauma, the first one I had ever experienced. I never thought such an experience could happen to me. I was plunged into terror and paranoia. My body reacted so intensely that I started thinking that the person I was with - and that I barely knew - might have given me a different drug than pot and my fear catapulted my anxiety level.

My body felt weak, my senses felt numb and I thought I would fall unconscious. I didn't know the neighborhood, but I ran as fast as I could to the nearest convenience store. I was convinced that the guy was going to chase me. It was like a horror movie. The employee there called an ambulance. Everything was spinning so fast in my mind and my breathing was fast and erratic. It felt like hours before I was finally transported to the hospital. I honestly thought I might die. For nearly five hours, I went back and forth between awareness and unconsciousness.

Once things settled down, I returned home, but I still experienced a lingering, uneasy feeling. I didn't feel like myself. I was drowsy and the physical objects around me didn't seem real. My vision was so wide, yet I couldn't focus on anything in particular. I felt like I was suspended in the middle of the air, and I was trying to remember who I was prior to that episode. It was frightening. I was scared.

Since nobody around me understood what I was going through, I searched online for some help, to find some answers. I stumbled upon a forum where a guy said that on some sensitive people, pot can act as a doorway to other states of consciousness. The same person then recommended to put all our faith and trust in God and pray for deliverance if we feel overwhelmed. That's what I did. After a long walk outside to breathe in some fresh air, I went back home and prayed with my heart to God for my fear and the unpleasant sensations to stop, and it did for at least two months. However, there was a greater purpose to this experience I was having, and I couldn't postpone my awakening much longer. Everything was happening in perfect Divine timing. When we are too stubborn to let our true inner core shine, the Light find a crack to let itself in...

CHAPTER SIX
The Awakening

After spending the March Break with my loved ones, I returned to school for another end of session and more exams. One morning, after spending the previous night studying, I went to class to complete my final test. I received my copy and while trying to concentrate on the questions, I started feeling spacey again. I was worried that I was going to faint in the middle of a class of hundreds of people, so I circled the answers quickly and immediately left the class. I just wanted to be in a safe place. I took the bus and went back to my apartment.

As the days wore on, I became more sensitive to the energies around me, and I started feeling a weird presence. This presence was so heavy and sticky that I felt suffocated.

About a week later, my whole awakening process reached a new level. After a long day at university, I went back home, cooked myself dinner, sat on my bed and then something strange occurred. I fell into a profound trance. When I "came back" to my normal state, I heard two words repeating over and over in my mind that I had never heard before. They were "shamanism" and "demonism".

Simply put, everything was happening to me at the same time and I felt on overdrive. I was awakening to my gifts, while some negative energies took advantage of my vulnerable state to mess with my energy. Of course, nothing ever happens without our consent, either consciously or subconsciously. I believe that struggling with poor self-esteem was contributing to attracting the negativity and what I was going through was also serving a higher purpose that I couldn't yet see or understand. The way I see it now, I was shown the two polarities of this world. "Shamanism" refers to the healing practice, while "demonism" expresses a lower vibration.

The fact that I had heard these particular two words in my mind was an indicator to me that what I was going through was spiritual and not a mental breakdown. My experience was accompanied by crawling and prickling sensations on my skin, vision distortions, mixed-up thoughts that did not seem to belong to me and many other abnormal symptoms. I returned online and stumbled upon many forums where people described their experience in similar circumstances. Some stories were not very encouraging and fed my anxiety.

If you are in need of assistance right now, I recommend finding a support group online or elsewhere. Find people with whom you feel a deep resonance, people that understand what you are going through and that can offer heart-centered guidance. And of course, working in conjunction with your doctor helps too as you may benefit from some medication, at least, until things settle. Do not believe everything you read or hear on the web because some sites want to scare you and you do not want to slow down your process of recovery. Your well-being must be your priority number one and you must cast your efforts towards restoring your health on all levels. The truth was that I wasn't psychotic. What was happening was real, and I was having a spiritual crisis.

I recall a reading I had with a psychic in the beginning stage of my awakening. Immediately, as we connected, she said: "Vincent, before going further I want to tell you that what I'm seeing is that your way of seeing life is changing. You'll never see life in the same way again, but this phase that you're going through right now will pass. A year from now, you'll be happy with the outcome."

Her words were reassuring to me on some level because I already knew the truth, yet harsh to my ego because it was afraid to change, to die. I believe that we "die" and are born anew many times in one life. I'm not talking here about physical death, but spiritual death. Our way of seeing life is altered through our various experiences and challenges. During this time, I did not want to change. After all, my life was going pretty well, or so I thought. I was succeeding at university, had a loving family, had a good place to stay and could work to make a living. Why would I want any of that to be affected? Talking to this woman helped me become conscious of the struggle with my ego, of my war with myself.

When June came, I returned to my parents' home for the summer. Lacking resources, and with my symptoms intensifying to the point where I couldn't leave my bed, I decided to spend three weeks in a psychiatric ward. I did that because I didn't know what to do to help myself anymore. I was suffering, I had panic attacks, and by this time, I knew there was a dark entity plaguing me. However, most of the doctors and the medical personnel said there were no such things as entities. I didn't find any help.

The truth is, I had become suicidal and I was drowning in a pool of harmful thoughts. I was afraid for the safety of my loved ones and for my own safety, because I didn't know what the dark entity could do, and I was empowering it through fear. I was prescribed two different antidepressants, an anxiety medication and a sleeping medication. I wasn't feeling anything anymore, but those pills seemed to keep me from doing the irreparable, so I recognized the need to use it, at least temporarily.

Thankfully, one of the nurses who worked there was a gifted individual and lightworker. I was blessed enough to have her as part of the medical team. We sat and I talked to her about everything I had gone through. That was a powerful moment. I felt safe with her, and I knew she wasn't judging me. In fact, she had gone through her own awakening.

She said: "Vincent, I'm not supposed to be talking about this in here, but you are not crazy. Mental disorder and spiritual awakening are two different things. I can see you in ways that some others may not. You have a bright, yellow aura. You are an old Soul. The difficulties you are facing right now will pass." Even though I was still in terror, for a moment I felt such a relief. Finally, someone understood me and gave me a ray of hope that things could get better.

Ultimately, this phase, that many refer to as the "Dark Night of the Soul", lasted for eight months. During this time, I tried different therapies and treatments. I was determined to find myself.

Just when I was about to run out of options, at least that's what I believed at the time, a friend of mine referred me a powerful healer. She helped my confused mind and hurting heart to understand what was going on and freed me from the negative influences that were affecting me. Most importantly, she guided me to the multi-dimensional vastness of my being and to the incredible power that lies within my heart. By regaining control of myself and by maintaining my intent to heal, I was then able to heal myself on a daily basis, and I've been dedicated to my spiritual path since that day.

After my healing began, I recognized other issues that I had to deal with, most importantly I could see that I had "awakened" a self from past life. That past self had died tragically and had not found his way to the light. He came to me because he didn't know where to go, and he needed recognition and acceptance in a kind of energy-filled embrace. My cousin and aunt, who are both clairvoyant, could see him around me. The healer I just mentioned later confirmed that this presence was, in fact, me in an earlier life and not a dark entity chasing me. Their confirmation helped me realize that we are so much more than we believe we are.

Many of us - and it's probably your case if you have felt compelled to read this book - are ancient souls who have volunteered to return here to Earth to help people during these ascension times. Each of us chose a physical form in order to accomplish a mission. We came here to learn and we knew that today's world would be the perfect setting to fast track our learning.

Even though my circumstances started to run more smoothly after this, I still had to heal myself numerous times when I dropped to low vibration again. More layers became conscious, and today I continue to learn different lessons and heal various aspects of myself. To plunge into the depths of your past is a process that requires patience, compassion and determination.

"The storm will shake you. It will break you, and it will sway back to you until all the lost aspects find their way back to the Light."

CHAPTER SEVEN

Overcoming the Victim Mindset

July 13, 2013 / "My story is pretty long but basically, a lot of spiritual things have happened to me in the last five months, and I feel very lost right now. At first, I thought I was 'awakening', but I've had so many bad feelings and thoughts about evil things just popping up in my mind that I'm afraid I'm being attacked by negative entities, and I don't know what to do to clear, shield and help myself…"

In my lost moments, I knew that suicide was not the solution, yet, on more than one occasion, during the extremely painful phases, I contemplated it. Thank God that I had angels and other light beings around to protect me. Somehow, I knew that there was no way to bypass what I was going through, not even physical death would give me a pass. I feared dying, and I feared living, so where could I go to find relief? At some point, I made a promise to myself, that I would keep going, no matter what crazy experience showed up in my existence. I decided to trust God fully.

When I felt completely lost, reaching out for help was the first step to hope and helped me to regain my power little by little. By sustaining an intention of healing every day and knowing within myself that there was a solution to every situation, I met with many people who turned out to be door openers in my healing process. However, I want you to realize that no one is meant to do the work for you. We are just guiding each other home. That others have helped me enables me to assist you in some way today.

Your healing starts with a thought and a deliberate action. Even when you think that you've tried everything and that there's nothing you could possibly do to save yourself, you always have the option to steer your life in the desired direction. No one's ever too messed up to help himself and the result of a willingness to change your life for the better will create opportunities that will likely surprise you.

One of the most empowering steps you can take is to be completely honest with yourself. Remember that we can't hide secrets from God. All of our actions and the intent behind those actions are seen as is the hurt we've felt caused by others. Even though we've convinced ourselves otherwise and buried painful memories deep in our subconscious, they are still there for God to see, and these hidden pains produce the patterns that we perpetuate if we don't deal with them once and for all.

At the end of your life, you will go through your life review. You will see where you followed your life's purpose and where you could have done better. Why not be completely honest with yourself right now, allow yourself to feel the pain, and clear anything that's standing in the way of your true self. Why continue to carry unnecessary emotional baggage? There is a huge amount of power that comes from being honest and true. When we live in integrity with ourselves and others, we feel no resistance, and we have nothing to hide, nothing to fear.

[Date unspecified] / "I feel so drained and am in mental, emotional, physical and spiritual excruciating pain. I have locked myself in a small room, laid on the floor and told my angels that the way

I'm living my life right now is exactly what I don't want. I just let go of everything, told them that I couldn't do this anymore and that I needed their help. For what? I couldn't even figure it out at that moment. Soon, I started to see a little angelic shape, and then they were two...and three. I just looked at the ceiling and saw the particles in the air more and more clearly until they came together, forming these silhouettes over me. I stayed there, without reacting, just watching them. I feel a bit better now, but I'm still so sad, tired and wiped out from being in an environment that does not support my creativity. On top of that, I'm still going through some painful steps of purging. I don't even want words of encouragement. I just feel like sitting with my storm and being with it, without expecting a single thing."

The point of sharing this with you is that I want you to realize that it's okay to be human and to experience meltdowns. Instead of criticizing yourself when you have one, learn to be present with it and see it for what it is - an indicator that something in your life must change. It's okay to allow yourself to feel your emotions. Feeling emotions allows them to flow out of you. You are then empowered to choose a different path for yourself.

Since the universe operates under the law of free will, even though God and the angels have our best interests at heart, we have to be the ones who make the right decisions, those that take us in the direction of our well-being. Like I said in chapter three, when my awakening occurred, I was dealing with a great amount of darkness. I had to learn a huge lesson about not giving away my personal power. When our choices are motivated by guilt, shame and fear from the past, either consciously or subconsciously, then these negative energies are exactly what we attract in our experience.

Manifestation does not happen only by wishful thinking, it's the art of embodying the vibration of whatever you desire and taking action where needed. This is why it is important to release anything standing in the way of Divinity. If you don't know where to start, ask your angels with an open heart to help you release anything that is no longer aligned with the Truth. Also, it helps to ask that they bring to your awareness any detrimental subconscious programs, so that you may let go of them. What you bring to sight cannot be hidden, cannot play tricks on you anymore.

The goal is to grow in awareness of the various aspects of your being. For every judgement you hold, every limitation you set, there is an underlying restrictive belief that you must get rid of if you want to further your process of enlightenment.

To overcome the victim mindset, it is crucial that you claim your personal power. Make the statement that you take back your power anytime you feel like you gave up on it in the past and present. Ask your angels that this vital energy remain clear and available because of the unconditional love and light of God. Take it back from anywhere it may have been and reintegrate it. That power is a natural and essential part of yourself, and it's nobody else's but yours. Do not be afraid to step into it.

You are a powerful creator. You are the co-creator of your life. When you clear your mind to unveil the workings of the Universe, you learn to use your power in a healthy and efficient way. There is nothing you cannot do or achieve. When you create healthy boundaries, free yourself, and start to emit your own energy instead of absorbing whatever is being thrown at you, a world of endless possibilities opens right in front of you.

CHAPTER EIGHT

Where the Magic Begins: Synchronicities and Their Hidden Meanings

Have you ever read a book or a magazine and at the same time you heard someone around you repeat the word you just read? Maybe you've recently asked a question in your mind and all of a sudden you saw a huge advertisement with the word "yes" or "no" or a short sentence that answered your question? Or you may have just looked at the clock and the time was 2:22, 3:33, or 4:44 for example? These can be signs from your angels wishing to catch your attention to communicate messages. The key is to learn how to interpret them, find out what they mean for you and how they relate to your present experience.

You may think: "What are these messages about?" or "I don't see or hear my angels, how can I know they are actually there?" The truth is, even if in this present moment you don't see your angels, they will always share their messages with you in a way that you'll be able to comprehend in that moment in time. All you need to do is formulate a clear question, ask them, ask that the guidance comes from God and the purest light, be open to an honest answer, be willing to step out of the way and then trust the guidance you are receiving in every shape or form. Also, use discernment as not every sign you think you receive are meant to be guidance. First, check how these signs feel to your heart. You will feel the truth intuitively.

As far back as I can recall, the number 4 has always been influential in my life. My earliest memory goes back to when I was in elementary school. Almost every year, I was number 4 on the alphabetical list of students in my class, and I rapidly identified it as my lucky number. Then, in my early teenage years, I started to catch the number 4:44 all the time on the clock. I wasn't sure why this reoccurrence was happening, but I already believed in angels then, and I had the intuition that they were trying to get my attention. I would pray to them, God and Jesus, and I felt comforted whenever I saw that number appear. I had a feeling that I was being looked after, that I was safe and protected.

I later searched out the meaning of the number 444 on the internet and landed on angel numbers and their definition. What I read about 444 confirmed what I had felt. Generally speaking, angel number 444 means that you are safe and that your angels are surrounding you with love. When I saw that, it was as if a new door opened for me. Simply by looking at numbers. I looked up numbers online, as they came to my awareness, to see how they were answering my questions at that particular moment. I was fascinated.

If you are wondering, like many, why you are not able to see, hear or feel your angels when you call upon them, the answer is simple. They vibrate at a different level than we do, so the more we align with that frequency, the more we are able to sense them. What's most important is to realize that they will always answer your call and to have total faith and trust, even when you don't see them, as this part is essential for manifestation.

The psychic abilities that allow us to enter into contact with the spiritual world are innate to all of us. The Divine is not something that is outside of us, we access it by tuning inwards. However, it may take time to be comfortable with that part of ourselves when we have closed ourselves to it. What I recommend is to clearly define your intention to perceive and feel your angels around you and to ask for help to release and transmute all that is blocking you from achieving this goal. Leave all fears in the hand of God and breathe. You can also repeat positive affirmations that support your intention. You will start to notice a difference.

As you practice opening up your psychic abilities, do not hesitate to seek the help of Archangel Michael for complete protection and visualize yourself in a bubble of white light. That way, you will feel much more confident, and you will ensure getting in touch only with beings of Christ Consciousness. Also, do not expect to see them just through your third eye. Be open to the ways they can make their presence known, such as: feelings, a deep inner knowing, thoughts, visions and, of course, synchronicities.

Here are some examples of synchronicities that I have experienced personally:

July 30th, 2014 / "Earlier today, I got a call on my cellphone from number 000-000-0000 and I thought 'Was it just a random number or does it have some kind of spiritual meaning?' At the same time I had that thought, the building where I live ran out of electricity and my cat jumped on my laptop keyboard and typed '45145'. So I looked up the meaning of number 145 and the description suited perfectly what I was going through in that phase of my life. How awesome is that? This is just one example of the tons of messages I get everyday, coming in many different forms, numbers being one form. I highly encourage you to be aware of signs as they are offering you guidance. You, too, are receiving them! Just open your eyes and your heart, the divine sometimes works in unusual ways from our human perspective."

July 7th, 2014 / "Last Thursday, I went for a drive and it turned out to be spectacular and majestic! On my way back, I started noticing repeated number sequences. In just a couple short moments, I saw car plates ending in: '222', '444', '777' and '888'. Later that day, I went to a restaurant and passed in front of a car ending in '000' and then, when I arrived at work, I parked right next to a car with the number '999'. I started to recall all the other number sequences I had seen that day and was amazed that there were so many different repetitive patterns. I sat at my desk, started working and my attention was drawn to the url at the top of my page that ended in '555'. I was shocked! Just a minute later, I saw a friend's status update simply as '3:33'. I couldn't believe it, I was ecstatic! Later that night, I caught '11:11' on my clock and then I thought: 'Wow! From all those numbers, there's only '666' I haven't seen today. I went to bed and the very next morning, upon waking up, I opened my cellphone to check if I had any new messages. Someone had messaged me the price of some items totalizing 6,66 \$. I couldn't believe it."

To me, seeing this suite of powerful numbers was symbolism signifying the completion of a cycle. Indeed, shortly after that, I started working on this book, and a whole new chapter of my life unfolded before my eyes. I started to emerge from the dark past of my life to a light-filled destiny.

I have felt like sharing these little stories so that you can see that once you open yourself to infinite love and let God's magnificence pulsate through your whole being, miracles abound to an extent that cannot be imagined or grasped by the analytical human mind.

Allow yourself to experience God's presence, and once you understand that it is real, then you will know that nothing is impossible, and your life will never be the same.

CHAPTER NINE

Remembering Who You Are

You are not your body. Your body is the vehicle that you use to travel in this three-dimensional reality. You, as a soul, chose it before incarnating on this planet. The universe is infinite. We, humans, are a species, but there are many more living beings everywhere in the cosmos.

As my awakening progressed, I became interested in discovering life on other planets, life in the star systems and life in other dimensions. I have found that there are many extraterrestrial beings accompanying us on Earth. Some of these are the Hathors, the Pleaidians, the Arcturians, the Andromedans, the Sirians and more. I began questioning myself about my origins of the intensity of my awakening experience. I started to ponder the possibility that I was not from here. Every single one of us is Divine, and our souls all come from God. I also believe that depending on the cumulation of our experiences throughout our past/other lives, each soul's growth is different and that there are souls that originate from elsewhere. That is not to say that one is better than the other. We are all equal in God's eyes and have our own purposes.

September 17, 2014 / "Is it possible to have your origins in more than one alien species? I ask this because since my awakening started, I've always associated myself with the Hathors based on a psychic reading. Then, I received a reading from another, gifted channeler who said I was a Pleaidian. At first, I discarded this new piece of information and thought she must have been wrong. However, the thought remained in the back of my mind, and the more I open myself to my divinity, the more I believe that this is not such a crazy idea. There must be a reason why I got two different answers. Everything is possible after all!"

The media and the movies associate fear with our big brothers and sisters, when in fact there is nothing to be afraid of. Indeed, not all aliens have our highest and best interests at heart, but they are only a small percentage. As long as we keep our vibrations high, ill-will cannot interfere with us.

The vast majority of alien species out there are beings of unconditional love and Christ Consciousness. They don't have an ounce of bad in them. They are here, monitoring the activity of the planet and intervening when they can, in Divine Timing and in accord with our free will.

As I said, as I explored my past/other lives, I discovered a strong connection with an alien species called the Hathors. They have been assisting human beings in their evolution for eons. They are sound healers and their power resides in their hearts.

One night, I was discussing something with a friend online, and I saw that she had many pictures and postings about the Hathors on her page. As the conversation unfolded, she said: "They are going to help you a lot in your journey." At the same time, I started to feel warmth in my whole body and especially in my hands. I was stunned.

A couple days earlier, I had seen a light energy around me and without understanding where this energy had come from, I felt it was them, I showed my friend the drawing I had made of that shape, and she strongly felt it was them as well "Their energy cannot be mistaken for something else", she said. As we continued to chat, I talked to her about the warmth I was feeling in my hands, and she replied: "They are reminding you of your energy-healing abilities."

Immediately after that, I felt a change in pressure in the room, and the lamp on my night table started to dim without my hand touching it. It remained in a dimming state for about 10 or 15 seconds before returning to normal. They were showing me that I wasn't imagining all of this. The spiritual can also manifest its presence in the physical. After that night, I started to believe in my abilities, and this event changed my perspective of myself and of the world around me.

At first, I really wanted to know where I had come from and which starseed I am. I know many of us have similar questions. However, as I advanced on my path, it became clear that it did not matter much. We are so much vaster and deeper than our human minds can conceive. What is important is to be present in this now-moment. Only then can we get glimpses of the vastness of our Soul.

December 30th, 2014 / "I seem to have hit a brick wall in terms of understanding a particular concept. So apparently our soul can inhabit many bodies. Let's say for example that Charlie, Adam and Keith are the same soul in essence, just different streams of consciousness. What occurs if something 'bad' happens on some level to Charlie? How could Adam and Keith not be affected if, truly, their soul is shared. I'm confused. I can grasp the fact that I, Vincent, have many personalities on one level and that I can choose the one that's best suited for a given situation. I also understand that I am multidimensional and that at a deeper level, I have many other parts to my Self. I am more than just 'me'. But I don't understand how Charlie, that I met on the street, can be me as well. I can't control what he creates out of his experience here on Earth nor can I control how this will affect my/our Soul.

I believe it is true that one Soul can incarnate into many different forms at the same time, and be more than one species, with different life contexts. We may also have incarnations in this dimension and others in parallel dimensions. The bottom line is, our Soul has chosen the perfect settings for the lessons it has to learn and the missions it wants to accomplish. I first remembered this when I was about 6 or 7 years old. I was in the shower and all of a sudden, I saw many "me's" in different dimensions at once. I quickly closed the vision because it was overwhelming, but today I understand that I was seeing myself in different timelines that might best be understood by imagining the layers of an onion.

Speaking of "time", time is a human creation. It is a system useful to create structure. However, the present moment is all there is. So that explains why all of your other lives are happening at the same time and that you don't clear something from your "past", it stays with you in the now. I know this may seem like an abstract concept, but it is not something to be grasped with the mind, it can only be understood with the heart.

Ultimately, if you feel that you are from somewhere else and that you have an important calling, then go within and ask. The answers you will get for yourself will be the most accurate. If it makes perfect sense to you that you are from somewhere else, then there is a reason for this.

"Child of the Universe"

Like a phoenix, I die and I rise
From the ashes of my past, I begin
My heart crashes from the sky
And lands in this beautiful tragedy, "life"

With meditation, I awaken
My indestructible spirit.
Time cannot stop me,
I am a Child of the Universe.

Let's come together as one
And dance 'til the stars go out.
Let's find within ourselves
A stronger, deeper, higher love
With which to fill humanity
With which to give a second chance to those who need it.

I pray that in every soul faith is restored,
That every teardrop fills an ocean of consciousness
That will expand the vision of love
So that everybody can find shelter
A glimpse of hope, a sweet memory
Even on the darkest side of night.

Let's come together, together as one,
Children of the Universe,
No melody's sweeter than the one we rehearse.
At the speed of sound,
We'll flip this world around.
We'll shake the grounds, and the skies,
Find peace in one deep, eternal breath.

CHAPTER TEN

Standing In Your Power

June 25ᵗʰ, 2014 / "I'm starting to feel better. I've been feeling very 'off' for the past couple days. I wasn't sure if I was afflicted by an entity, fatigue, the incoming energies or all three! Regardless, I knew that the only way through this situation was love and the absence of fear. I have said my usual prayers and talked to God, the angels, Archangels and Ascended Masters. When I trusted that I was safe, I lay down, kept visualizing myself in white light and surrendered to the healing and purging of negativity. I repeated this a couple times over three days and I'm now starting to feel the shift. I experience no more fear. I just need to recover my energy and focus. I also feel that whatever was 'there' is now gone, even though I'm still releasing the remnants of it. I'll keep reaffirming my intention, I'm a strong warrior!"

Standing in your power is one of the most important things you must cultivate daily. The definition of "power" might not be the one you have in mind. It's not about having control over anyone. An empowered being is one who has learned self-love and then teaches others by example. There is a distinction to be made between people using their power negatively by taking advantage of others and those using their power gently to impact humanity in a positive way.

No matter what your life mission is, it will require you to stand in your power and have confidence in your heart-centered convictions. Reaching an empowered state requires a healthy balance of affirming and letting go. You must know who you are, and what you want, and be willing to fully trust the Universe to support you.

Personal power is about learning to set clear boundaries. Some beings, both physical and nonphysical, will be attracted by your light. It is important that you affirm to yourself and the Universe that you only allow God's unconditional love and light into your space. You may do this whenever you feel more sensitive, a couple times throughout the day. It is especially important as you go to sleep, before going into crowded places, before performing an energy healing or before connecting sexually with another being. Otherwise, you might pick up on vibes that are not yours and start to wonder why you feel so heavy and drained.

July 28, 2014 / "I feel like I've opened up a lot. I'm able to heal myself now with the help of the angels and I've made many positive changes in my life. I'm monitoring my thoughts daily and great things are manifesting very quickly in my life. Right now, I feel that I'm on the verge of a breakthrough. I'm shifting into a different state of awareness in meditation. I'm allowing myself to see parts of this new reality, then I block it because it seems so vast, and I experience the fear of the unknown. Then, I notice the fear and return to awareness. This situation is daunting. How to fully trust, when what you're about to see is so different from anything you've seen in this incarnation? I feel like I'm at the top of a huge diving board, about to jump into the vast waters, and yet, I have to remain still, trust and just let myself go. I'm afraid that by opening my heart more, I will also open up to things that are not in my highest and best good."

Spiritual protection and energy clearing exercise

Spiritual protection and energy clearing should be important parts of our everyday lives. In my experience, I've found that our energetic clarity is directly linked to our capacity to use our free will. When we set energetic boundaries, we ensure that only what is aligned with our highest and best good can reach us. As energy beings, we are affected by everything around us. If we don't shield properly, we can become vulnerable to all kinds of energies present around us. These energies can cause confusion, anxiety, loss of vitality and even hinder our personal power. This is why it is so important to use spiritual protection regularly, which then enables us to open up the heart space. In this section, I will share with you some exercises to assist you in this practice. First, here is a channeled, guided meditation I have written for this purpose. Just relax and read through the healing words.

"It's been a long journey. out of the madness and into a new perspective. I know what you've been through, for I too, have walked a thousand miles in these shoes. I've been looking at you from a distance, but I was never far at heart. You had to climb this mountain to realize just how strong you are. Today, I am here to tell you, that you've made it through. I am here to help you remember who you truly are.

Your feet might be sore and your heart cold, but don't let the troubles of this world tame your wild soul. You are a shining star that landed in this beautiful tragedy called life. You are going up, pointing the way for those ready to reach new heights. Do not doubt. You came here with all you needed in order to accomplish this mission. And nothing you could ever do or say can change this fact. You are more powerful than words can express. Your essence cannot be contained nor bound.

You needed all of your experiences in order to grow, both the positive and negative. Yes, even this one. You now come from a place of honesty with yourself, and affirm that you are stepping back into your personal power and free will, without excuses. You choose to see the powerful being that you are. You acknowledge that the unpleasant situation you are facing right now has served its purpose.

We declare that we are ready to release what is holding us back. Now is your time to break free. Take a deep breath. We ask Mother Earth to ground us so that we have stability, peace and clarity of mind. We ask the rains from the heavens to wash over us and clear us from all the stress, worry, fear and anxiety we've been feeling. The bright golden-white drops feel warm on our skin and permeate our whole being. The rain fills us with a deep sentiment of being nurtured and cared for. The mild wind embraces us gently with love. We enjoy this moment so much that we take the time to breathe in deeply once more, just being present with what is.

Allow yourself to release resistance. The sooner you do so, the quicker negative attachments will be shed. You must allow the light in to create the proper environment for healing. We now call upon Archangel Michael and his legion of angels. We ask that they cut cords and attachments to any and all negative energies, lower thought forms and dark entities. We send those immediately to the light, for healing and transmutation.

You see Archangel Michael's Sword of Truth spinning all around your energy field. It's made of light so pure that only what is aligned with your highest and best good can remain. All the rest is escorted to the Source by a band of benevolent angels. You now visualize all of your being surrounded and filled by white light. You are able to see clearly and effortlessly all of your energy field. If you notice, with your mind's eye, some places where there are still clouds of darkness (including roots, webs, wires, belts), simply take the Sword of Truth and remove them confidently by yourself. You can then fill the gap with pure light essence.

In the future, you will be able to repeat this as needed. There is no point in fearing anymore. You realize that fear is an illusion. See how easy it was? You healed yourself, you did it! Let's take a moment to relax and let the healing energies sink in."

There are many ways to clear your energy, one of them is to visualize the pure white light of God all around you with your mind's eye and then see it become fuller and brighter. If you are unable to see it in your mind or have trouble visualizing, I suggest that you ask your angels help you clear anything that is standing in the way. Sometimes, these blockages can be feelings such as doubt or insecurity and at other times, they can be attachments or entities. It's not so important to know exactly what the cause is, as long as you allow the purging to occur. In any case, your angels will help you to clear anything that does not belong to your space and empower you to heal yourself energetically. I used to experience the same frustrations, but when I started grounding myself, breathing and asking for help, things started to change in the most miraculous ways. I really encourage you to do the same!

Like I mentioned in the guided meditation, I highly recommend using Archangel Michael's Sword of Truth. Once you've surrounded yourself with the light, just envision a big white or blue word spinning around your energy field. If you attune yourself to your field, the space inside and around you, you'll be able to see exactly where the cord is, otherwise just continue visualizing and this will ensure that any dark attachments are shed.

Then what I do is I visualize a portal of light coming down from the Source and I ask angels to escort the attachments to the light. Once a negative entity has gone to the light, it cannot come back to you.

However, monitor your vibration to ensure to keep it high. Getting caught up in negative thinking patterns attracts dark energy which then empowers our fear.

When in need of a quick cleansing, simply imagine the pure white light of God pouring like a waterfall from the skies and flowing through your whole body from head to toe. See the liquid light permeate your being and wash away all lower vibes, and you will feel lighter instantly.

Protection before going to bed is also important. When we rest, we leave our physical body and go into other dimensions. We are always connected our body by an unbreakable thread, nonetheless, spiritual activity tends to be accentuated during the night. Some lower energies might see this as an opportunity to do harm. This is why it is so important to protect ourselves before going to sleep. It can be done in numerous ways, but this prayer for night time is effective:

"Dear Archangel Michael, I ask that you stay with me at all times, especially right now as I prepare to go to rest. Thank you for surrounding me with your protection. Help me to be peaceful in the knowing that all is well and that I am safe. May you remove any and all negative cords from my energy field and your presence dissipate harsh energies. Only God's unconditional love and light is allowed into my space and it is so."

These powerful affirmations that promote self-love can also act powerful shields against unwanted energies. When we vibrate at the level of love, nothing else but love can approach us:

- I am a powerful being and I stand in my power.
- I embrace myself fully and completely.
- I am awake and aware.

- God's energy fills me and surrounds me. I am protected by this strong light.
- I allow joy and love to fill my heart.
- I give permission to my inner child to express himself freely.
- I allow myself to love again.
- I am blessing to this world.
- I allow myself to have faith and trust again.
- I am open to the help and guidance of angels and light-beings of Christ-consciousness.
- I am enlightened, all fear vanishes.
- I can now say that I love myself.
- I strive to make this world a better place, starting with me.
- I stand in awe of my own magnificence.
- None of my past experiences define me.
- I am free. I am freedom.
- I am prosperity and abundance.
- I enjoy this life to the fullest.
- I am safe, I can relax and let go of all tensions.
- I explore my talents, passions and interests.
- I give love free of expectations.
- God sees this world as perfection, so do I.
- I create the life of my desires. I am a powerful creator.

Loving yourself and experiencing joy and gratitude for the world around you are also important parts of your power. When we see ourselves and our surroundings in a positive light, we are then more empowered to express ourselves in creative and uplifting ways.

CHAPTER ELEVEN

The Upheavals You Might Experience in Relationships

March 22nd, 2014 / "There are lots of angels around me these days... They are making their presence known. I see them very clearly appearing around me... It's great because I really need them in this transition. I'm not scared. I'm just exhausted and "normal life" continues without anyone around me noticing... How strange!"

August 14th, 2014 / "Is it normal that the more I advance on my spiritual path, the less I tend to connect with some other people? I feel like I need to retreat and be with myself... Is it wrong that I enjoy spending most of my time alone? I can't seem to stand human energy for too long. Sometimes, I try to avoid engaging in conversations with people because they're too absorbed in the material world. They then think I'm rude or that I don't care... Should I try to engage with others more?"

It is important to remember that your life is changing in many ways internally and that this will have a direct impact on your circumstances, especially your relationships. You must embrace your path while still honoring others' journeys. Sometimes, some people's energy might feel harsh to sensitive lightworkers, however, it is important to set energetic boundaries and do your best to be compassionate. Remembering that we've all been through various stages of development helps us to embrace and accept others exactly as they are. No one is better than anyone else, we are just at different stages in our individual development.

There is a saying that we are the sum of the people with whom we spend the most time. In a way, this is true. One thing is sure, we attract the people who are currently vibrating on the same wavelengths as us. Every single person we meet is a teacher. When we react strongly to another's personality, this means they've hit a truth cord. That truth cord is an indicator that there is an inner aspect needing to be embraced and healed.

What happens if we disagree with others and can't make them see our viewpoint? Sometimes, keeping words inside will be more detrimental to yourself in the long term. If this is the case, find a way to express your truth in a loving way. Otherwise, simply silently send his or her words to the light for healing and bless the person with love. This way you become in control of your life and are not influenced by a program that did not belong to you to start with. If you must, open your heart and tell God how you feel. This will help to regain balance and inner peace. Be mindful not to absorb other people's fearful ideas. Fear is learned. The goal is not to find fault but to consciously choose what thoughts to nourish and which ones to dismiss.

Other people's energy affects us and the more time we spend with people who carry negative energy, the more we tend to absorb it and repeat their patterns subconsciously. Energy awareness in relationships is important. Do not hang on to friends that do not understand or support your path, but instead follow your heart and surround yourself with people who accept you as you are.

Have empathy for those who speak from fear. They, too, have been exposed to some form of conditioning and have learned their behaviour from somebody else. The goal is not to find fault but to consciously choose what thoughts to nourish and which ones to dismiss.

Be compassionate. When you find yourself in a process of transformation, it's already complicated enough, for you flow through changes, so imagine how hard it can be for others who don't yet have the awareness to grasp what is happening to you. Don't expect them to understand, or you'll feel discouraged. The best way to deal with a lack of understanding is to take some time for yourself and let others be. Let them think and say what they want because you have no control over that. Resistance leads to suffering. Those who are meant to stay in your life will stay. It might even surprise you who stays. Your relationship might and will probably change in the future as a result of your awakening. What remains important is that you treat others with respect no matter what their understanding of your current situation is, despite your frustration.

Some might think that you've completely lost your sanity. They just want you to be like you were before because it suited them better. These fears do not belong to you, but if you react in an egotistical manner, then your behaviour adds to the problem. It might take a while understanding how to relate to others, so have compassion for yourself. Remember that if you're "flawed" from a human perspective, at a soul level, you are perfect no matter what you do or say. Just act with your heart and the heavens will see your intent to do good.

When it is not possible to have an open conversation with another individual because both egos are clashing hard, simply retreat, and release the tension, anger, frustration and resentment you are feeling towards that person until harmony is retrieved. A better outcome to this kind of conflict will be possible if you manage to rebalance your emotions. Self-awareness is necessary for a positive resolution. It is your responsibility to monitor your thought patterns and emotions.

CHAPTER TWELVE

Healing the Inner Child, Addictions and Karma Clearing

You have spent part of your life unaware. Unaware of the laws under which this world operates. Unaware of your vulnerability to potentially painful energies. Unaware of the hereditary nature of belief systems that affect everyone unconsciously. Now it is time for you to release the conditioning. Be aware of what you believe and what energies surround you.

Now, let's talk about how the pain body influences our addictions. When the pain body stores a traumatic memory, it creates an energetic trigger, and when that particular trigger is pushed, the person runs toward a certain substance or behavior as a way of suppressing the pain temporarily. Remember that ascension is about balancing all aspects within the self that have not yet found peace.

The release of addictions is a tricky subject, but ultimately it starts with an intent to forgive yourself and others for everything that might have caused this addiction, and understand that at a soul level you are a perfect being in the image of God and that only from an ego standpoint can you be at "fault." Then you must ask for help with an open heart, from God and from your angels. Be at peace knowing that for them, anything is possible, and they already know what's best for you. You can say a prayer like this one:

"Dear God, the Archangels, my angels, guides and other beings of unconditional love that are currently assisting me in my journey or that are willing to offer their healing energy right now. I ask that anywhere in my past and present where I still have the memory of _____, be released to the light for healing and purification. Furthermore, I now clear in the name of God and Jesus Christ (or replace with the deity of your choice), all negative effects of this trigger, in my past, present and future."

Then, visualize your whole body being surrounded in pure white light and breathe. If you are like me, you might start to cough very deeply or experience other physical symptoms. That means you are clearing blocks, and you are doing a great job. Do not expect an outcome in particular. Just set an intention, open to the healing energies and repeat as needed. When you experience setbacks, be kind with yourself and remain aware of all the feelings that are coming back to the surface. They must be experienced again before they are finally released.

Although the healing of an addiction can happen suddenly, for most people it can take a while, and the healing process is an individual process that is not a straight line. Don't be hard on yourself if you go back to the addiction. In my journey, I've found that keeping a journal to write about my feelings or praying helped to soothe my emotions and relieve the stress and anxiety I felt. Another thing that helps me is keeping an "emergency sheet" near me where I list all the reasons why I want to part with a certain addiction or behaviour, reading it can act as a reminder.

Karma clearing also is an essential process on the path to your divinity. The reason is simple, you cannot embody your full potential while you are still holding onto the negativity of yesterday. All the pains, suffering and limiting beliefs you hold are blocks to the realization of yourself. It is very important to release all the negative thoughts, feelings and patterns from your memory so that you don't keep attracting the same things over and over again. Energetically, you attract what you vibrate.

It's very easy to spot what our patterns are and to ask for help in releasing them. Some may take more effort than others to clear, but it's worth it. An exercise to help you do this is to observe your actions on a given day and take note of your recurring thoughts and impulses. Karma clearing is important to balance unresolved issues within ourselves. Clearing karma doesn't mean a universal principle is erased. Clearing karma means you are aware of a pattern in your life and you eliminate the necessity to repeat it. I understand karma as a philosophy of life consequences resulting from an individual's behaviour. The consequences may even follow from the actions of previous lives.

Here are some ways you can use to clear karma. Have a journal that you will later destroy and write out the painful memories. The goal is to purge the memories that are binding you to the past. You can also release karma with prayer and intention, by talking to God and Archangel Michael for example, and asking for specific (or more general) painful things to be removed from your energy or balanced from your soul's history. In my experience, this is a lengthy and gradual process. Combining the techniques has proved the most beneficial to me. It is possible that when you do these exercises, your body reacts strongly or you have violent dreams afterwards This means that you've successfully cleared an issue that no longer served you.

Many of the restrictive patterns we develop stem either from guilt, shame or fear. Don't put a time limit on how long your healing journey will take, because you will need to get to the root of the problem before it is completely cleared and balanced. However, contrary to what you might think, it doesn't have to take hours and hours of long and deep shamanic trance to resolve your issues. Thinking that healing might take you forever could discourage and keep you from doing any inner work. Remember that if it's simple, it comes from Spirit. When it's too complicated, it most likely comes from ego. That's an easy, basic rule to remember that will help you discern the path you choose in the future.

The purpose of reliving some unresolved situation from the past may be so that you can acknowledge what you have learned, embrace this lesson and allow yourself to purge. Repeat the process as needed. Once your state of being is again harmonious, you will feel an inner sense of peace, and you'll see a definite change in yourself.

August 5th, 2014 / "Last night, I did an inner child healing and went through a deep emotional purging. Then, in the middle of the night, I woke up from a dream and saw an eye symbol with fire all around it. This morning, my neck is very sore, and I can barely move my head. I wonder what all of this means…"

The night before this, I had visited my parents, and we had viewed some old tapes that my mother had filmed throughout my younger years. After a particularly rough day at work, I needed some comfort, and I think my mother sensed it. I don't go into the past often, unless it's to release a memory or to revisit a pleasant memory. But that night, seeing the tapes turned out to be exactly what I needed to do some introspection.

Looking at the younger version of me, from a baby to later on in my childhood, I experienced a complete shock. The little boy I saw was so vibrant, full of energy, charming and had such a natural sense of humor. It's right to say that I fell in love with myself all over again, seeing my true essence radiate. What I was seeing in the footage was the real me. Not the drained, detached and jaded version I had become through hardships. I told myself it was time for change.

I then felt the urge to do a guided meditation on healing the inner child. I highly recommend doing this experience. You will know when the time is right for you to do so. I felt such a profound release. I was only two minutes into the meditation when I couldn't stop crying. Anything that stood between me and the purity of my inner child came up for release. it was a humbling experience.

Healing the inner child is an ongoing process, a quest we should all be on - even when, like me, you've had a happy childhood. It liberates us from anything that no longer serves us, anything that is not aligned with our innocence - our essence - throughout all of the past, throughout the various phases of life.

Remember that the child often doesn't know how to shield himself from negativity and process through emotions. nor does he see a need for it, because he's unconditional love and unconditional love is where he comes from. So when he experiences his first rejections and when someone is mad at him because of something he did, the wounding is more direct than it is later in life, when the young adult learns not to take things too personally. The child experiences his first doubts and believes that "he's not good enough". He then desperately seeks validation and this behaviour extends into other relationships as he grows up, until the issue is addressed internally and heals. That's why as an adult, you must learn to take care your inner child. With patience, you will make peace with that part of yourself and vice versa. Harmony and joy will be achieved.

When I feel sad, as funny as it sounds, I lie down and caress my belly and my chest. That's my way of reconnecting with my inner child and sending him love. And, at the same time, I say a positive affirmation such as: "I love myself and all of Heaven loves me", and it helps me find peace, comfort and reassurance.

The Ho'oponopono technique

The Ho'oponopono, an ancient Hawaiian technique, is an effective way to clear past hurts. If you've never heard of it before, it's a popular technique that can assist you in forgiving yourself and others. It consists of four statements that have a profound effect when repeated over and over. To perform a memory cleansing using the Ho'oponopono technique, you can say either out loud or silently the following sentences: I'm sorry. Please forgive me. I love you and I thank you. As simple as it might seem, these statements hold so much truth and vibrate on such a high level that they break down patterns and fill space with pure love.

A word on "sin"

Many of us hold onto guilt because we falsely believe that we have sinned in the past and that what we've done is unforgivable. This is a false belief. In fact, there is no such thing as sin in the way we understand it. Believe it or not, in God's perspective, there is no "right" or "wrong". Everything just is and serves a specific function in the bigger picture. Every experience we have in our lives is a cornerstone to our development. No action is at fault. We need not judge our actions. Every living being serves the same God and represents a piece of the whole. Of course there are universal rules by which we must abide, such as the Law of Karma or the Law of Attraction, which ensure that we draw to ourselves what we give out. In other words, we cannot hurt others without hurting ourselves. However, the consequences of our actions are the result of cause and effect, not a punishment from God.

We are one, even though we forgot this when we incarnated here. We are here to remember. There is no one more or less divine or better or worse. Jesus and the other Ascended Masters who once walked our Earth loved unconditionally, and that's what they came to teach us during their time here. Conditional love, on the other hand, labels, judges and puts restrictions. It is not aligned with the highest truth. Conditional love is a kind of love that comes with expectations.

Most relationships nowadays are based on conditional love and this is why there is so much dissatisfaction. When we live with expectations, it indicates that there are aspects of the ego to be transformed before we are able to live from the heart. However, when we give freely, without wanting anything in return, we can only feel deeply fulfilled. To finally break from the cycle of reincarnation and live forever freely in the unconditional love and light of God, we must get rid of all darkness keeping us attached to duality and to lower realms of existence.

"Away in the Clouds"

Away in the clouds, I will shine.
Weather the storms, sway through the wind to carry on.
Like a ray of shine piercing through the darkness,
I will find a way to make it out of this mess.

Snowflakes are melting on my face,
From ice to water are dissolving those mistakes I embrace.
Lost in the vastness of the ocean,
My senses are numb, but my heart is pulsating through my being.

I cast away the burdens of yesterday
And welcome the fresh air
I accept all that's been

And salute my courage,
Standing in awe of my own magnificence.

Cracked are my hands, but full is my Soul.
The journey of lifetimes takes a toll.
A crash in the infinity of the unknown
And all that remains is this simple song.

CHAPTER THIRTEEN

You Are Neither A Body, A Gender, Nor A Sexual Orientation

You are not a gender nor a sexual orientation. You are not even a body. You are boundless love. You are a blend of masculine and feminine energies, inhabiting a male or female body in this lifetime. Our society has taught us of the love between a man and a woman - which is a beautiful thing - but let's not forget that this same pure essence also manifests in many ways, shapes, and forms. One of this is the loving relationships between two men or two women.

Your romantic and sexual preferences, if any, have been determined before your incarnation for specific purposes. If you think that this idea is inconceivable and against nature, ask yourself how it makes you feel inside to hold such a judgement. As you do, you will notice the feelings of constriction and heaviness in your stomach and heart. Such a feeling is far from love. How you feel is your indicator of what is aligned with your Higher Self and what is not.

You might also want to review your beliefs about monogamous relationships, including the "need" for marriage. While some people may find happiness in marriage, not everybody should have to follow the same mould nor have the same needs. We need to drop the labels and accept what is God's will for each and every one of us. When we judge another, we are in fact judging God's perfect creation, and that is the product of inner turmoil. Judging another means that there are still parts of ourselves stuck in denial, seeking their way back to the light. When we embrace all of those parts of ourselves, we are then free to experience the wholeness of our being that some desperately seek outside themselves.

Ultimately, all is God's creation and carries His sacred flame. Be open to explore all that you are - that untamable torrent of love that is not bound by any of the programming from the dark ages. And remember, as long as you act with love, you can never go wrong.

The iBully Era

In 2011, I participated along with other students in a theatre play called "iBully". The goal was to raise awareness about the issue of bullying in schools. We each covered a different aspect of bullying by writing a monologue that expressed what we personally had gone through. One monologue was about being bullied during childhood, another one was about sexual abuse, and mine was about the homophobia I endured during high school.

Still today, nothing equals the feeling I had walking out onto that stage and voicing out loud my story. After all those years of being ashamed of my identity because of judgement, I stepped onto that stage and said everything that was on my heart. Still today, I wonder how I was able to do that without crumbling or my voice cracking. After all, I was experiencing so much anxiety and depression at the time. I believe I had many angels around me boosting my self-confidence and comforting me. I felt it was my calling and when one of my teachers offered me the opportunity, I accepted. I was meant to do that!

Nothing could have prepared me for the reaction. Each time I presented my monologue, I received a standing ovation, and I say that without pretension. Some of my persecutors even came to me afterwards to apologize for what they had done to me. A complete shock. They shared that the way I explained what homosexuality was, had changed their way of thinking. I still have the chills writing about this. We then went to present the play at a festival, and we won many prizes for our participation. I was also interviewed by a local journalist with my parents and our story was featured on the front page of that newspaper. It was a huge step for the cause of equal rights in our community. Needless to say, the play was a success, and we accomplished our initial mission.

This memory will remain forever in my heart. At only 17 years old, I did something that was directly aligned with my soul's purpose, and I'm proud of that. It was such a defining moment in my life that, that I decided to join to this book the monologue I wrote at that time. I spoke my truth. It came from my the heart, and I believe this message is timeless. Even though, with the awareness I have today, I would probably rewrite some parts, I have only slightly edited it so that you can feel the emotion and hear the message I wanted to tell at that time.

"One day, I understood that judging somebody is, in fact, having an idea about someone without knowing where they came from. This is a problem in everyday life that we all must face. A judgement is the result of entertaining false ideas about someone. Ignorance causes us discomfort. We judge and we lost the potential for connection.

I was bullied for all sorts of reasons, always the same reasons these monsters could use to justify the fact that I 'deserved' such harsh treatment. It was an extremely difficult period of my life. Adolescence can be quite challenging as we all search for identity. While I did not yet know who I was, some felt justified in excluding me, persecuting me because I seemed different from them. Everyone knows that difference is scary. But what makes me so different? What is so disturbing about loving someone of the same sex? Am I a failure? No.

Do you know what it is like to live in constant fear? To feel your stomach in knots as soon as you walk into school? Do you know what it's like coming home and crying until you're sick? So you know how it feels when you're all alone against a group of thugs who constantly want to torture you? I just wanted to go unnoticed. And if they saw me, what kind of treatment would they inflict on me? In my darkest moments, I wanted to get rid of the life I had come to believe I didn't deserve. My level of confidence was reduced to dust while my fear of others persisted. The moments of happiness that I lived, I could not even enjoy because I had no trust left in life whatsoever.

For years, I saw the scenes scroll through my thoughts like a bad dream resulting in severe anxiety disorders and depression. What saved me was having exceptional parents and friends to count on. Out of respect for them, I did not give up. I told myself that my life was worth living if they loved me. My psychologist helped me to use the hatred which lived in me as fuel to forge ahead. The only way to heal is to deal with it.

Lately we have heard the most terrible stories in the news. Stories of unspeakable sadness about young homosexuals who have committed suicide due to pressure from society due to their sexual orientation. In three words, here's a life lesson that we must spread widely: 'Love is love.' Whether it is between a man and a woman, two men or two women: True love is the one that comes from the heart. It is the foundation of everything that exists. Without love, there would be absolutely nothing that surrounds us right now. So why destroy the love between two people?

I learned quite a lot during those difficult years while I was bullied. Now, I understand that the value of an individual is not touched by the judgements that are around him or her. I realized the importance of my own existence in this world, and I will never let someone bring me down again. I breathe, free from the chains of my past, ready to find the future, one that matches my aspirations. I am ready to show the world who I really am. I'm not a failure; I am intuitive, creative and sensitive to my surroundings. I'm not weak, I have convictions that I defend, and I have the fire of life, of love that's burning inside of me. It is this passion that fires me, and I am ready to burn down all the barriers in my way. To traverse new horizons. I'm proud to be me. Proud to be Vince. Proud to be gay.

Today I stand up to represent myself and the entire gay community. We are human, and we are all born free. We were born who we are. My goal today is not to impose my lifestyle. Instead, I want to open your eyes to a world where we welcome differences with an open mind. A world where it feels good to be, where all the prejudice can fall into oblivion.

Some people do not understand the true meaning of love. To be loved, we must first know how to love unconditionally. I offered myself the greatest gift, the right to love. The only important thing is that the word "love" finds its meaning in the presence of the person who shares your life. I hope these words will echo: soothe the troubled souls, sound like a comfort to the ears of those who supported me and give courage to those who recognize themselves in my story. I speak today for all the times I should have. Scars don't have to hinder our future."

CHAPTER FOURTEEN

Releasing the Shame & Guilt in Sexuality

One of the main themes I have had to deal with in my life, and I feel that it may be the case for many, is the shame and guilt revolving around my own sexuality. Even though I didn't have difficulty accepting my sexual orientation, as it felt natural to me, expressing my love and sexuality freely with a partner was and still is a struggle at times. I now understand that it stems from a lack of self-worth. Hearing people invalidate my path during my teenage years certainly didn't help, but I feel my fear stems from issues from past lives.

Whether you are male, female, straight, gay, bisexual, transexual or identify yourself to some other category, no one escapes cultural conditioning. Dark energies can use guilt to grow. Many are told that sex is "not before marriage', that it's "between a man and a woman" or maybe even a "sin". One thing is sure, there is a lot of negativity and repression attached to the subject of sex.

It is the responsibility of each and every one of us to release the shame and guilt we carry with respect to our sexuality, both at the conscious and subconscious levels. As we ascend spiritually, all the negative beliefs we have held on to must come up for healing.

Fantasies

Your sexuality is one part of who you are. Your sexual preferences and fantasies are part of your imagination, your creation. You should not be ashamed of your fantasies. You might want to experience these fantasies or not, depending on their nature, but if a fantasy is recurring in your mind, no matter how uncomfortable it can be, observe it from a distance and don't get caught up in the guilt. If it ties you up in dependence, and you feel unhappy with it, it is likely that it stems from an issue in a past life that has not been resolved before physical death and forgiveness was not found within this self. Some memory has been stored at an energetic level, and you have another chance to clear this imbalance within yourself.

You need to acknowledge the sexual part of yourself and treat it with love and respect, just like any other part. You cannot ignore your sexual identity, block yourself from seeing it and still fully embody your divinity. That's not how it works. If you keep shaming yourself for your sexual preferences, then there is still healing to do. Once you come from a loving place of self-acceptance, you are empowered to choose what's best for yourself and stay away from what would be detrimental to your well-being. A fantasy, however, can take a long time to fade away, if it ever does fade away, so be patient with yourself. It's a constant work of making conscious choices that will align with your soul essence.

Ask your angels for help with this as many of us carry harsh memories related to our sexuality, whether we are aware of them or not ; whether they come from this life or another. As hard as it may be, always make an effort to see the bigger picture. All perceived challenges in life serve a purpose and propel our soul's growth. Each path is unique and peace can always be found.

CHAPTER FIFTEEN

Trusting the Divine and Following Your Life's Purpose

[Date unspecified] / "I'm going through another rough patch, feeling very depressed and I keep meditation but it seems to get worse. I need help. I need a break. Going to see my doctor on Monday and I wonder if I should ask her for a week off or not. Devoting my life to my 'job' like I do and not having time for anything else is definitely part of the problem and unhealthy. I'm starting to think that this anxiety and depression is something that I'm going to have to fight in cycles all my life, because I'll never be able to quite find my place in this world. I find it so difficult to be here on this Earth. It's like I just don't belong and I can't bear people's judgments. I know that we ultimately choose whether or not to let others affect us, I know that we are the masters of our lives, but some circumstances are so difficult to go through."

I started to notice angel numbers around the age of 16 for the first time, but it was really after my awakening at the age of 20 that my awareness expanded, and that I started to notice more and more of those numbers. I looked up the meaning online of various repeating numbers I was seeing. They were pointing me in the same direction - I needed to start my own spiritually-based career. Even though I had no clue where to start, I let the Universe be my guide, and I started to receive more and more signs in order to assist me on my path.

I have started by writing this book about my own experience of spiritual awakening. I have launched pages about spirituality on social media. I have built a website where I share articles and my passion for psychic readings and energy healings. With each step I take, I am guided to the next.

[Date unspecified] / "I'm making the courageous decision that I won't let a corporate job steal my fire and prevent me from fulfilling my inspiring spiritual purpose in this life. Change is to be expected. I won't let anyone stand between me and my dreams, nor will I allow limiting beliefs to deter me. I can do this. I don't yet know how, but I will. I can have abundance, even more than in my wildest dreams, if I open myself to it and give no other choice to the universe, but to make this happen. I am worthy of spending the rest of my life doing work that I'm passionate about, and by doing so, giving my best in service to others."

I had a writing job in an environment that was very stressful to me at the time I wrote those words. Also, I felt that what I was writing about wasn't helping others the way I wanted to help them. Other people might have found themselves to be a perfect fit for that job and find happiness and satisfaction in the position, as there were definitely some aspects and benefits I enjoyed. But overtime, the stress of performance and having to meet tight deadlines started to weigh heavily on me. I felt depleted and drained mentally and emotionally.

I took some time off from work and started to work on this book when I could, while resting and healing. My mind was telling me: "You're crazy. Don't do that. They will lay you off and what are you going to do then without a stable income?" But my heart and the guidance I was receiving were saying: "Now it's time that you think about yourself and all the other people you are going to help by writing this book. If not now, when?"

Today, I can say that if I hadn't taken that break and hadn't started writing this book, then you would probably not be reading it right now. I'm glad I followed my intuition. Sometimes the Divine guides us to make decisions that seem so illogical, but the lack of logic doesn't mean the decision is not the right one. Of course, it is important to use discernment, but sometimes taking a leap of faith is what is required for things to start shifting in a more positive way.

[Date unspecified] / "I am now on the most challenging yet breathtaking path to fully trusting the Divine. I'm experiencing changes and guidance that I simply can't ignore. It seems like I can't go against that wave of love at all and I don't want to resist it either. To surrender your being and drop your self-imposed limitations, to completely trust in God and your soul's purpose is a humbling experience. I can imagine some opposition, but I release it to light because that's not what I want to create in my reality. I just want to be me... entirely. The real me. No more hiding, no more pretending, no more fitting inside the boundaries set by others. I am living my truth. I am a powerful lightworker. Yes, this is who I am, truly. And all the growth I've experienced in my life has led to this moment. It is now the time to embrace who I truly am, and it feels scary but I have a strong spiritual team with me and precious friends on Earth to guide me through. God has carefully prepared me for this day and there is nothing holding me back anymore. I have shifted enough, that the rest will take care of itself. What's next, angels? I am ready to accept my mission and pursue my calling."

When you follow your divine path with passion and speak your truth confidently, as beautiful and inspiring as the journey is, it can sometimes stir fears and doubts inside people who have closed themselves to the magic of life a long time ago. They then feel the need to voice out loud their opposition, to invalidate your journey and to argue to prove their point. Remain still and present. Let them be, and bless them even when they've been hurtful to your gifted soul and sensitive heart. Remember that their reaction is an ego reaction and that is never truth. The ego always seeks to distract us from our essence, and when we are not aware of how it works, it controls us with lies and judgements and keeps us in denial of our nature. Take heart, as all of this is just a reminder that what you do is very much needed by the world, and you are to pursue your path with grace, knowing that God and all the benevolent light beings of the universe support you in your endeavours.

CHAPTER SIXTEEN
Opening Your Natural Gifts

Sept. 14th, 2014 / "Something incredible happened today! A friend was doing a reading for a young lightworker and she asked me for help. She said that she felt thrown off because there was intense energy around the other girl. So I said: "How can I help?" And she asked me to send healing energy to the young lady distantly. At first, I wasn't sure how to do it, but I felt prompted to try regardless. I started by surrounding myself with protection, and I connected with intention to the person's energy field. I visualized her in bright white/golden light and sustained that vision like I do when I heal myself. Then, also through visualization, I started to spin Archangel Michael's Sword of Light around her field to clear any negative attachments that might have been there. When this was done, I felt guided to bring Source energy through my body and send it from my heart to her. While I did that, I visualized the angels taking balls of dark energy out of her, and right afterwards, I saw a cord linked to a dark entity in my mind's eye. I used the sword again to cut the cord, and I opened a tunnel of light from the sky and the angels immediately escorted the dark entity to Source/God. As the negative entity left, I saw its image appear in my mind. I reaffirmed my intent for protection and then cleared some more remnants of negative energy in her field and asked the angels to finish the healing work and repair her aura if it was needed. I wasn't completely sure if it had worked or if I had just 'imagined' this and my ego was challenging me. After all, I had done the healing work from a distance and without establishing physical contact, without even knowing what that girl looked like. I asked my friend, and she confirmed that the girl had felt the energy shift and the negative energy leaving her. We then had the chance to talk to each other, and she explained that she felt my energy and then felt the dark finally leave and it was such a relief to her. I'm still in awe! What a beautiful experience. That gave me the confidence to believe in my innate abilities. I am very happy to have helped create a positive difference in someone else's life."

I believe that everyone is capable of unlocking his or her innate psychic and healing abilities to assist themselves and others. However, this "unlocking" is a process and requires a sustained intent and extensive healing. Most of us have wounds from past experiences in this life and other lives and when they are not healed, then we become more out of touch with ourselves and our natural gifts.

Some people open up psychically at childhood and stay connected to their abilities throughout their lives, while for most of us, it takes time and determination to break through the blocks to our divinity. Ultimately, these spiritual gifts are to help humanity and everyone awakens to his own gifts when the timing is right. No path is the same and not everyone is meant to become a psychic in this lifetime. If you feel compelled to develop psychic abilities that you feel you have, then rest assured that the angels will assist you with this process.

Sept. 16th, 2014 / "Yesterday, a friend came to me because she needed assistance and healing sent to her. I didn't have more information, so I connected to Divine guidance and asked how I could help. I released the need to figure everything out right away and quickly had three visions afterwards: Her heart, tears and a male figure. I asked her if her issue was related to the loss or departure of a man in her life. And she then explained her loss. She felt she had lost the heart connection with her lover, a man she considered to be her twin flame, and she was grieving that loss. This then helped me to personalize her spiritual healing session. I coughed intensely for about 30 minutes. I focused on her heart chakra since her loss was emotional. At first, I doubted myself a bit, but then I asked her if she had felt my energy and she replied: 'Oh God! Yes, yes, yes! I feel it, dear! I am finally feeling the energy and love of my twin flame, who is constantly with me in spirit. You have no idea how grateful I am.' After that, I slept for four hours! I really need to be careful with my energy and take good care of myself when I do this kind of clearing, because it's demanding energetically."

Your life's purposes were established before you arrived here on Earth. You have an important mission, to bring more love into this world and to help others heal, starting with yourself, but there are also things that only you can accomplish. Your goal is not to find yourself a life purpose, but instead to remember the one you came here with.

A life purpose can be anything from loving your family members more deeply, to helping other people in certain areas of their lives, to breaking a certain pattern that you might have been carrying around for a while. Anything that will make your soul grow and that will be of benefit to yourself and others. A life purpose will often involve a talent that you have that will beautify the world in some way.

How to find the field in which your expertise is needed, is quite easy. Think of your passions, interests and the problems of this world that you feel particularly drawn to change. These are not coïncidences. For example, I've always liked to write, and I've discovered that a part of my mission is to help others awaken spiritually and heal by writing heartfelt articles, books and poetry on the subject.

I have also enjoyed music since my childhood. Writing music and singing are other parts of my mission. As I'm aware that many find symbolism in songs and can relate to lyrics and melodies, I also share music from my favourite artists daily on my online profiles. An example of how this has benefited others is what happened the other day. I had shared a particular song just because I liked it and found the lyrics meaningful. Right away, two of my friends commented that it was exactly what they needed to hear at that exact moment. I was shocked! The universe works in mysterious ways.

Another thing I feel compelled to do is to defend the rights of lesbians, gays, bisexuals and transgendered individuals. I want to raise awareness that we are not so different. At the end of the day, you love who you love and you are who you are. We are all come from the same God and long for love.

It is up to you to find your calling and what your heart longs for. Only you can figure that out for yourself. Your mission consists of a variety of small to bigger things that make a difference in this world. Deep within, you already know these things are what will make your soul and the world ignite.

CHAPTER SEVENTEEN

Keeping Up the Faith and Raising Vibes

September 17th, 2014 / "I went through such a powerful healing and release this morning. I was guided to go read about the Laws of the Universe. I read them all, and it gave me so much perspective into the world we live in and into the natural laws under which we operate. I was able to reflect upon my own path and understand where I went off track and how I had to readjust for the future. I invoked and activated some healing through prayer. I then felt an energy so powerful flow through me, to an extent I had not experienced before. It was purity. The angels, Archangels, Ascended Masters and the Universe were assisting me in releasing all the unnecessary burdens and karma from the past. I revisited some people from my past and asked them for forgiveness, forgave them, blessed them with love and sent anything negative to the light for healing and transmutation. I did this with an open and genuine heart, and the pure energy kept intensifying, especially in my heart. When this was all done, I slept for ten hours straight and dreamt so much. I feel that this is the beginning of a whole new life ahead of me, and I am very grateful for how everything is unfolding in my life... Thank you!"

No matter how you do it, reconnecting to the Source daily is essential to staying happy, vibrant and on the right path. Whether it is through meditation, or through a sacred ritual or prayer, it will give you the faith and strength that you need in order to keep moving forward with your life.

When things are going too fast, and we barely have time to breathe, it's easy to become disconnected from the core of who we are. It's during these times that we tend to indulge in patterns, behaviours and addictions that do not serve our highest good. The reason we do this is to numb the pain that we are feeling inside and to give ourselves a renewed sense of joy, although it always wears off quickly, often leaving us more depressed than we were before.

After all, what do we truly need to survive? Not much when we think about it. I'm certainly not saying that we should all become monks and dismiss the little extras that we might find enjoyable in this lifetime, but the problem arises when our lives become ruled by these distractions. I think it's important to find time to get in touch with our deepest selves and to see what is healthy, what we need to balance and what we need to get rid of.

I want to help you incorporate more awareness into your daily actions and remember that balance is key. Balance is what helps our systems (physical, emotional, mental and spiritual) to naturally heal themselves. As always, remember to be loving and compassionate with yourself at all times, but especially in periods of transition.

I always emphasize compassion for ourselves and for others in my teachings, especially while we are going through some behavioural changes. Old ways might take a while to change, and we all have an inner critic that's very good at pointing out our flaws, mistakes and patterns. Knowing this feeling all too well, I try to bring as much peace, harmony and understanding to others as I can to help them neutralize the inner bully and focus on their goals.

At times, keeping our act together might seem like an impossible stunt. If we keep at it, the positive effects will ripple into our future. God gave us another day on Earth because he believes in us, so as long as we're breathing, no matter what kind of difficult situation we might be facing right now, we still have an opportunity to make things better. Maybe not in the way we have envisioned them, maybe differently. We must avoid judging things as being right or wrong and just move along.

CHAPTER EIGHTEEN

Maintaining an Attitude of Gratitude

Aug. 15th, 2014 / "I went to a drive-thru yesterday, and the woman who worked there, I feel, has battled many addictions and demons in her life. Still, everytime I see her, she's very positive and makes an effort to smile. I know just how difficult her job can be, and I felt compassion for her so I gave her the change in my pocket to express my appreciation for the great service. I did not expect her reaction. She was overwhelmed with gratitude ! She shared that she was saving to get a puppy. You could see the stars in her eyes and just how happy she was. For me, it was just some change, and for her, it was a piece of her dream. It felt good in my heart."

The quality of our lives is determined by our perception. An attitude of gratitude is so important to manifest the most auspicious circumstances in our lives. I was first introduced to this concept in 2011 when I started reading a book on gratitude. At the time, I was working at a campground for the summer and when there were no clients, which happened at different times of the day, I would sit down on the bench outside to read and practice what I had learned. One writing exercise was about being aware of all that I already had in my life and listing it down. I took the time to write my blessings.

At first, my goal was to find ten reasons to be grateful, from the most simple things, like the air I breathe, and the roof over my head. I immediately noticed that for each item, there were more reasons to be happy. For example, by being grateful for the park where I often go to walk, I became grateful for the trees that surround it, for the peaceful atmosphere and for the butterflies that fly around. When you think about it, there are tons of things to be grateful for everyday. We need only correct our mindset to recognize them. The more you devote yourself to this practice and see life for the beauty that it really is, the more things just seem to fall into place for you, and the Universe sends you more reasons to be grateful.

I started reading the book on gratitude right after I came out of a very difficult heartbreak, and I needed something to hold on to. The pain I was experiencing was unbearable. Anyone who has loved deeply and then lost can relate to this feeling. However, the way I see things now has considerably changed. I believe that this heartbreak too was divinely planned, as this heartbreak then awakened something inside of me.

My sadness made me realize that even though I'm a romantic person, I could never find happiness with another man if I was not at peace with myself first. Finding peace is something I'm working on every day. When I reflect upon my past experiences, it's as if all the pieces were coming together. My soul was sending me challenges so that I could wake up and start to work on myself.

When I started to adopt a more positive outlook on life by expressing gratitude for what I had, I saw circumstances shift in magical ways in my life. I started to feel joy and gratitude in my heart to such an extent that the joy lifted my pains and struggles for a time, until I stopped practicing gratitude daily. The reason I stopped feeling joyful was quite simple, the wound was still there, and I needed to release the trigger of my pain to retrieve harmony.

A while ago, I saw a video of a guy on the internet that expressed what I was learning in a very cool way. He took a bottle of water to which he added a few drops of black food coloring until the water turned dark. Then, he started to pour clear water into the already full bottle. This resulted in some of the black water overflowing but still, most of the water remained black for a few minutes until only clear water filled the bottle.

The lesson is that you must be persistent with your intent. Of course, you will experience setbacks along the way, it is part of the process. As long as you see the setbacks for what they are and realign with your path each time, you will come out stronger and wiser from each experience. With experience comes depth. It is not to be feared. It is to be embraced.

Finding a Lost Object With the Help of the Divine

One morning, I was about to leave home for work and I couldn't find my car keys. I had used them the night before and for some reason, when I woke up, they were nowhere to be found. It was so unusual that it almost felt as if someone had hidden them, yet I lived alone in my apartment. I thought: 'I'll call a taxi to go to work', but my debit card was also locked in my car.

I had to go to work that day, and I absolutely needed to find my keys in order to do so. After looking everywhere in my apartment, and starting to feel anxiety and panic, I decided to breathe, let everything go and ask for guidance. By turning inwards, I could see my angels and guides, and I kept asking for help, but I couldn't get a clear answer yet. I was trying too hard, resisting. Secretly, I had lost hope that I would find them. So I thought: "You know what? I trust you entirely and completely to show me where they are. If not by vision or thought, you will find a way. The universe always provides !

After that, I lay on my bed and closed my eyes for a couple minutes because I was exhausted. When I woke up, I opened my laptop, and my cat jumped between my arms, put her paws on the keyboard and typed the letters "h" and "n". So I asked: "Is there a meaning to that?" And immediately, the thoughts "house" and "night table" popped into my mind.

Until that point, I wasn't sure that the keys were in my apartment. I believed they might have slipped from my pockets in the driveway or in the street somewhere. So I pulled over the night table next to my bed and found nothing underneath it. I got discouraged and thought I was imagining all of this. Then, I flipped the table 180 degrees and discovered, for the first time, that the back of the table had an open space. It was designed in such a way that an object could easily fall in there. So I reached inside and found my keys! I was in awe of what had happened.

This is one example to show that with intent, as well as complete trust in the Divine, and action where required, it is possible to attract what it is that we need.

Becoming a Great Energy Reader and Spiritual Healer - FAQ

I'm often asked: "What makes a great reader?" A great reader is someone who is able to transcend his own ego and attune himself to receiving higher truths being transmitted by Spirit. We are the instrument of God, the channel through which information flows. To provide a clear reading, the reader must be in a place of openness and be fully willing to receive guidance from the Divine. That is why it is so important for us to find a protection ritual that we feel comfortable with and keep our vibration high, so that we only attract energies that are aligned with the highest and best interests of all concerned. Also, a great reader is not a prophet of bad news and should use discernment and integrity while doing a reading. Although we might see negative things and offer them as possibilities to give a broader spectrum to the client, it does not mean that they are set in stone. I am a firm believer that life is not just "happening" to us all. Life is what we make of it, and we have the power at each passing moment, to change anything that is no longer aligned with our truth. I want you to realize that you have within you all you need to create anything you wish for and desire in this life. The rôle of the reader is to empower you to become the unlimited potential that you are inside and to guide you to your next best steps with regard to your life's path.

"Is charging money for a spiritual service wrong?"

Many gifted souls keep themselves from achieving their goals because they worry that charging money for what they do is not aligned with God's will. This is just one of the many insecurities that we face once we have made the deliberate choice of stepping outside our comfort zone and sharing our gifts with the world. Seeing money as something negative is a false belief based on old fears that no longer serve us. Money itself just "is". It is not "good" or "bad". In charging for our service, we exchange energy with someone. Finding fault with the exchange is a judgement. The Divine understands that in this reality, we all have a physical body to take care of and so, it is correct from a spiritual standpoint to ask for a financial contribution in exchange for our work. I'm writing this for the lightworkers that are holding back their innate gifts because they fear doing something wrong. Do not let money be a stop to the expression of your Divine abilities. You chose to incarnate here because the world needs you. Take all the necessary steps to ensure that you are able to fully devote yourself to your mission and always work from the heart.

"Why invest in a reading, healing or other spiritual modalities?"

Investing in a reading is investing in yourself and your future. You are actually opening yourself to the possibility of a better tomorrow. Personally, I have never hesitated to get a reading or a healing from someone with whom I resonated, and they have always proved to be of great benefit. God and his angels always make sure to give us exactly what we need to move ahead. This gift then enables us to reflect upon new truths and develop a new way of seeing life. They say that each dollar you spend is a vote you are casting for the kind of world you want to see, and that is 100% accurate. Think of all the money you may be spending on meaningless stuff in the material world. One of the greatest secrets of the happiest and most successful people in the world is that they put time, money and energy towards their passions, talents and skills through which they expand, flourish and grow. They believe and know that they are worthy of the money they earn, and you should know this to be true for you as well.

Printed in the United States
By Bookmasters